PRENTICE HALL D I

MW00716956

EXPLORING
THE POSSIBILITIES

Boston, Massachusetts
Upper Saddle River, New Jersey

Copyright © 2007 by Pearson Education, Inc., publishing as Prentice Hall, Boston, Massachusetts 02116. All rights reserved. Printed in the United States of America. This publication is protected by copyright, and permission should be obtained from the publisher prior to any prohibited reproduction, storage in a retrieval system, or transmission in any form or by any means, electronic, mechanical, photocopying, recording, or likewise. For information regarding permission(s), write to: Rights and Permissions Department, One Lake Street, Upper Saddle River, New Jersey 07458.

Pearson Prentice Hall™ is a trademark of Pearson Education, Inc.

Pearson® is a registered trademark of Pearson plc.

Prentice Hall® is a registered trademark of Pearson Education, Inc.

ISBN-13: 978-0-13-363643-7
ISBN-10: 0-13-363643-7
1 2 3 4 5 6 7 8 9 10   11 10 09 08 07

PRENTICE HALL DISCOVERIES

Exploring the Possibilities

How much information is enough?

Table of Contents

FORENSIC ANTHROPOLOGISTS

Giving a Face to the Past

Everybody knows what America's first president looks like. George Washington stares out at us from each and every dollar bill. On the money, Washington is fairly old and very dignified. This is the way we picture him in our minds.

But what did Washington look like earlier in his life, when he was a child or a young man? It's hard to imagine what a young George looked like because no such pictures exist. At least they *didn't* exist until very recently.

This wax model shows a 19-year-old George Washington. It stands in the new visitor's center at Mount Vernon.

Today, over two centuries after Washington left office, we finally have a fuller picture of our first Commander-in-Chief. Thanks to the hard work of some forensic anthropologists—scientists who study and identify human remains—and the magic of advanced technology, **accurate** 3-D models of George have been constructed. They show him at three different stages of his life.

"3-D George" is just the tip of the iceberg when it comes to reconstructing the past. Forensic anthropologists are using new technologies to take on the **challenge** of history's mysteries and put faces on people who lived centuries or even millennia ago.

3-D George

The effort to recreate George Washington began at a museum, Mount Vernon Estates and Gardens in Virginia. The museum was the president's former home. He lived there from 1761 until his death. Today Mount Vernon Estates is **devoted** to helping visitors learn about the former president and his world.

Vocabulary

accurate (AK yuh ruht) *adj.* free from error; correct; exact

challenge (CHAL uhnj) *n.* something that tests strength, skill, or ability; an invitation to try to defeat someone in game or a fight

devote (di VOHT) *v.* set apart for a special use or service; dedicate

As part of a new education center at Mount Vernon, museum directors wanted to create three life-size sculptures. The sculptures would show Washington at three different ages. They would show him as a young man of 19, as a 45-year-old soldier, and as a dignified leader of 57.

Creating figures like these is usually an easy task. Artists find photographs or portraits of the subject at the appropriate age. They **obtain** the details they need to **capture** his or her appearance. In this case, however, the **research** was going to be much harder. Photos obviously were out of the question. Cameras didn't exist in Washington's day. Neither, however, did portraits or drawings of the president as a young man.

Without these images, making the sculptures was going to be difficult. That's why the museum looked for an expert to **assist** them. The person they chose was Jeffrey Schwartz.

VOCABULARY

obtain (uhb TAYN) *v.* get something that you want, especially through your own effort, skill, or work

capture (KAP chuhr) *v.* succeed in showing or describing a situation or feeling using words or pictures, so that other people can see, understand, or experience it

research (REE serch) *n.* careful, systematic study or investigation of a topic or field of knowledge

assist (uh SIST) *v.* give help to; make it easier for someone to do something

This photo shows the garden at George Washington's home near the Potomac River in Fairfax County, Virginia.

Mystery Solver Schwartz is an anthropologist at the University of Pittsburgh. He knew a lot about solving mysteries. He had worked in a coroner's office examining dead bodies. He had spent his research career studying early humans.

Schwartz looks at bones, skulls, and other remains, and then tries to determine details about what people were like. To recreate the president, Schwartz would need access to his skeleton. Since no one was going to dig up Washington's remains, Schwartz had only a few pieces of **evidence** to work with.

One was a set of dentures. Like many people of his day, Washington had begun losing teeth as a young man. Another was a pair of eyeglasses. A third was a bust, a head-and-shoulders sculpture of the president created when Washington was 53. A fourth was a life mask—a molded cast of the president's face. It was made at the same time as the bust. There were also a few items of clothing the president had once worn.

Tech Tools Schwartz realized he would need some advanced **tools** to help him with his task. One was a 3-D digital scanner. Ordinary scanners are two-dimensional; they only scan flat objects. 3-D scanning would **enable** Schwartz to do impressive things. For example, he could scan the president's dentures and insert them into a digital image of the head. Then he could figure out the curve of Washington's jaws.

Schwartz used 3-D scanning to measure the life mask and bust. The mask he knew was accurate. It was a mold of the president's face. The computer measurements

A young boy looks at examples of research exhibits in a "forensic laboratory" at the Mount Vernon Education Center. The exhibits describe how scientists and artists determined what George Washington looked like.

implied that the bust was accurate, too. Schwartz was **impressed** by the sculptor's accuracy. More importantly, now he could **rely** on it as he continued to **investigate** the president's appearance. He continued building his digital image with details taken from portraits of the president as a middle-aged man.

VOCABULARY

evidence (EV uh duhns) *n.* facts, objects, or signs that make you believe something exists or is true

tools (TOOLZ) *n.* any implement, instrument, or utensil used to do a particular job

enable (en AY buhl) *v.* give someone what they need to be able to do something

impress (im PRES) *v.* have a marked effect on the mind or emotions of someone

rely (ree LY) *v.* trust someone or something to do what you need or expect them to do

investigate (in VES tuh gayt) *v.* search into so as to learn the facts

9

Schwartz relied on the help and talents of many colleagues. One who **participated** in the project was imaging specialist Jeremy Hansen. Hansen wrote a computer program to transform the digital image of the older Washington's face to a younger one.

Schwartz and his partners were **fastidious** about every detail—from creases in the skin to the length of the earlobes. Earlobes grow throughout your life. A younger Washington would have had shorter lobes. He also would have had a fuller jaw in this period because he had not yet lost his teeth.

Artist Stuart Williamson stands between his unfinished life-size wax models of George Washington. On the left, Washington is shown as the 57-year-old president. On the right, he is shown as a 47-year-old Revolutionary War general.

Body Work Once he was satisfied with the head, Schwartz moved on to the body. The staff at Mount Vernon Estates provided him with 18th-century clothing that Washington might have worn. He examined the size and fit of the garments.

In recreating the body, Schwartz applied his knowledge of how bodies change at different ages—what happens as a young man grows older, for example. He made **credible** assumptions based on historical facts. If Washington had bad teeth, for example, he probably ate softer, fattier foods. This **implied** that George had probably fattened up substantially in later life. Schwartz used this sort of **criteria** to project the changes in Washington's body shape over time.

In fact, Schwartz used the sum total of his anthropological experience to put together all the evidence. The digital bodies were joined to the digital heads. Now, on computer at least, one could **appreciate** how Washington must have looked at three different stages of his life.

VOCABULARY

participate (pahr TIS uh payt) *v.* take part in an activity or event

fastidious (fa STID ee uhs) *adj.* not easy to please; very critical of anything crude or coarse

credible (KRED uh buhl) *adj.* believable; reliable

implied (im PLYD) *v.* suggested

criteria (kry TIR ee uh) *n.* standards or tests by which something can be judged

appreciate (uh PREE shee ayt) *v.* recognize and be grateful for; think well of; understand and enjoy

Artist Sue Day puts the finishing touches on the model of 19-year-old George Washington.

Transforming these images into physical form took several steps. First, the data was sent to a team in California that created life-size foam heads. These were turned into molds. The molds were then used to make new heads out of clay. Artists used wax and paint for the finished work. To **infuse** the heads with even greater accuracy, they were topped off with human hair.

Finally, the heads were attached to foam and plaster bodies and clothed in articles that Washington would have worn at each age. Thanks to the talents of Schwartz and his team, and the high-tech **devices** they used, visitors to Mount Vernon can now see something special. They can see the evolution of George Washington from an ordinary young man to a soldier to a world leader. Now that's something that a dollar bill could never hope to **illustrate**!

Teaming Up for Tut

Jeffrey Schwartz is not the only forensic anthropologist giving a face to the past. Three teams of scientists, one Egyptian, one French, and one American, recently finished a job with a similar **focus**.

VOCABULARY

infuse (in FYOOZ) *v.* put into

devices (di VYS uhz) *n.* techniques or means for working things out

illustrate (IL uh strayt) *v.* make the meaning of something clearer by giving examples

focus (FOH kuhs) *n.* the central point of a work

Their subject was even older than George Washington. In fact, he had died more than three thousand years ago. He was the famous Egyptian ruler, King Tutankhamen.

King Tut's mummified body was found in 1922 by archaeologist Howard Carter. Carter and his crew wanted to get a better look at the **disheveled** mummy, so they pried him loose from his container and mask. To do so, they cut him into pieces with hot knives, damag–

Until the teams of scientists used high-tech devices to study King Tut's mummy, this ancient statue gave the best idea of what he might have looked like.

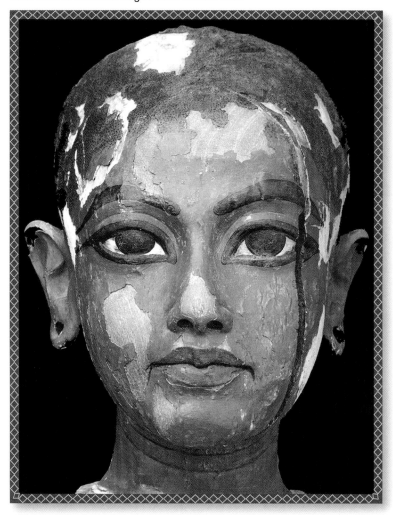

ing the body. This made it even more difficult to learn anything about how Tut looked—until now.

3-D Scanner Like Schwartz, these scientists were assisted by high-tech devices in their work. Unlike Schwartz, however, they were able to use the physical remains of their subject. Tut's mummy was removed from its Egyptian crypt. It was then sent through a modern medical scanner.

The scans revealed a great deal about ancient Egypt's king. They **suggested** that Tut was less than 20 years old when he died. His physical development was not complete. His wisdom teeth had not yet come in.

The scans also cast doubt on the long-held belief that Tut had been murdered by a blow to the head. A lump on his head that had been used to **support** this theory was determined to be nothing more than resin used for the **preservation** of his body.

Finishing the Face Hundreds of 3-D images of Tut were taken with the scanner. Details enabled researchers to do something previously impossible. They were able to distinguish between damage done to the mummy by Carter's team and injuries Tut had suffered while alive. The details also allowed researchers to reconstruct the boy-king's face.

VOCABULARY

disheveled (di SHEV uld) *adj.* untidy; rumpled

suggest (suhg JEST) *v.* show indirectly; imply

support (suh POHRT) *v.* provide evidence to prove or back up an idea

preservation (PREZ er VAY shuhn) *n.* the act of keeping something unchanged or unharmed

15

The three teams worked blind; they were not able to see one another's work. Yet, while the final reconstructions differed slightly, each illustrated Tut's appearance in a similar way. He had a baby-face, wide eyes, an overbite, and an unusually long skull.

It wasn't possible for the researchers to figure out every detail from the scans. A scan cannot provide evidence of eye or hair color, for example. Still the researchers overcame centuries of **ignorance**. For the first time in more than 3,000 years, people have a good idea of what the ancient Egyptian boy-king looked like!

The Mysterious Men of the *H.L. Hunley*

Yet another researcher who combines anthropology and technology is Douglas Owsley of the Smithsonian Institution. In 2006, Owsley began to investigate a historical mystery involving ordinary men. The focus was a group of Confederate sailors—crewmen on a Civil War submarine named the *H.L. Hunley.*

On a February evening in 1864, the men set out on a secret mission. They sailed the sub toward Charleston, South Carolina, and blew up a Union warship. The feat was a first—no submarine had ever sunken a warship in battle.

The sailors, however, never got a chance to appreciate their accomplishment. The *H.L. Hunley* also sank—shortly after the warship!

VOCABULARY

ignorance (IG nuh ruhns) *n.* lack of knowledge or awareness

Confederate reenactors march in front of the Confederate submarine *H.L. Hunley* after it was raised from the seabed.

Confederate reenactors carry the remains of the *H.L. Hunley* crew before they were taken to the *USS Yorktown* to lie in state.

More than a hundred years later, the *H.L. Hunley* was raised from the seabed in Charleston Harbor. While the sub was well known, mystery surrounded the remains of the eight men on board. Their mission had been top secret, so no information about them had been recorded. Who were they? What were their names? What did they look like?

Surprising Discoveries For Owsley, answering these questions was the challenge. He got busy, using forensic science and old-fashioned detective work. First, he created a digital map of the soldiers' remains. Next, he began to analyze their bones and body tissue.

Some of his findings were surprising. The small size of the sub—it was barely three feet wide—had suggested that the sailors would be small. Owsley's study, however, found the opposite. The men of the *Hunley* were bigger than the average Civil War soldier.

Another unexpected discovery was the country of origin for some of the men. Chemicals in their bones implied that several had grown up in Europe and not in the United States. Owsley and his colleagues used personal effects, census records, and DNA testing to identify the men.

Today, the sailors have names like Dixon, Ridgaway, Wicks, and Lumpkin. They also have faces. Owsley worked with artist Sharon Long to complete facial reconstructions for each of the eight sailors. Visitors to the sub, now on display in Charleston, will soon be able to see what each of these early submariners looked like.

Learning About the Past Forensic science isn't new. People have been studying remains to solve mysteries for centuries. Eight hundred years ago, the Chinese scholar Sung Tz'u was examining bodies found in the water. It was easy to tell if a person had died by accident or foul play, he decided. Water in the lungs meant a person had died by drowning. The absence of water meant a murderer was probably on the loose.

What is new, however, are the technologies being used by forensic anthropologists. Whether they help us take a new look at an old president, put a fresh face on an ancient mummy, or identify long-lost Civil War soldiers, these technologies give us a glimpse into the past.

Discussion Questions

1. Why do you think people want to know what people of the past looked like? What does this add to our sense of history?

2. Why must forensic anthropologists make certain guesses or assumptions in their work? How does their knowledge of history, science, and human behavior help them make certain inferences?

3. Which recreation—George Washington, King Tut, or the men of the *H.L. Hunley*—do you think made the best use of forensic anthropology? Which one had the most impact for you? Explain your answers.

Scientists study the submarine to learn more about how the crew of the *H.L. Hunley* died.

Honoring Our Best in Every Field

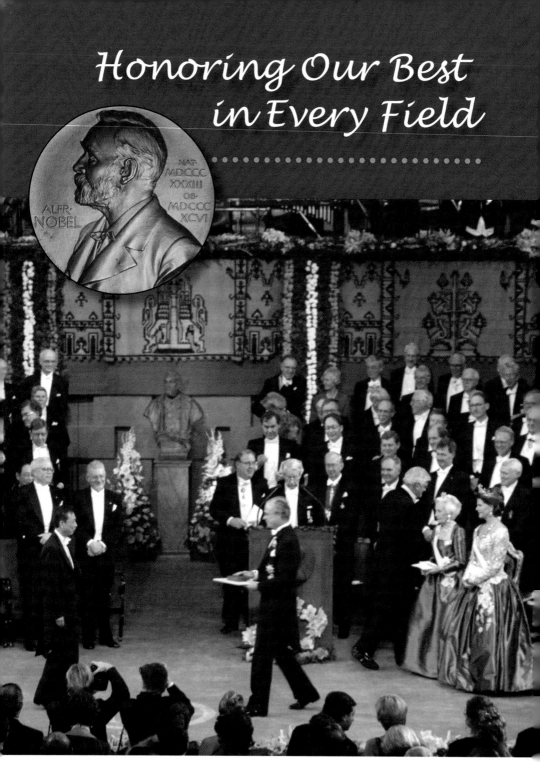

Each Nobel Laureate receives a Nobel Prize Diploma, a gold medal, and a large amount of money.

Have you ever thought that you would like to make your mark on the world? Would you like to be honored for inventing something that **benefits** people everywhere? Would you like to be known all over the world for a special achievement? Perhaps you'd like to **contribute** to ending poverty. Maybe you'd like to find a way to **minimize** aging. Many people want to do something to make our world a better place. Alfred Nobel, the famous inventor, decided to provide an **incentive** for people to do just that. That incentive has come to be called the Nobel Prize. It is awarded each year in the fields of chemistry, physics, physiology or medicine, literature, economics, and peace making. With it come worldwide honor and a lot of money. People who receive the prize are called Nobel Laureates. The award of money **enables** them to continue working in their chosen fields.

VOCABULARY

benefit (BEN uh fit) *v.* bring advantages to someone or improve their lives in some way

contribute (kuhn TRIB yoot) *v.* give money, help, or ideas to something that other people are also involved in

minimize (MIN uh myz) *v.* make the degree or amount of something as small as possible

incentive (in SENT iv) *n.* something that makes a person act

enable (en AY buhl) *v.* give someone what they need to be able to do something

23

Shared Nobel Laureates in Economics

If you saw the movie or read the book *A Beautiful Mind,* you already know something about one Nobel Prize winner. In the Oscar-winning film, Russell Crowe plays John Forbes Nash, Jr. Not everything in the movie is **accurate**. However, it offers some insight into one brilliant man's intellect.

In 1994, the real Nash won the Nobel Prize for Economics. He shared the prize with two other men:

In the movie *A Beautiful Mind,* Russell Crowe played the brilliant economist John Forbes Nash, Jr. This is the real John Forbes Nash, Jr.

John C. Harsanyi and Reinhard Selten. All three were awarded the prize for their work on the science of "game theory." Game theory guides everything from the questioning of suspects by police to the **fiscal** policies of nations. Some questions posed in game theory include *What do I know? What does my opponent know? What will he or she do? How does that affect what I choose to do?* The three men were honored for refining game theory.

Gabriela Mistral, Nobel Laureate in Literature

In 1945, Gabriela Mistral received the Nobel Prize in Literature for her poetry. She was the first female Latin American poet to win the prize.

Mistral was born in 1889, in Vicuña, Chile. She was of Spanish, Basque, and Indian descent. Mistral felt **compassionate** toward the poor and oppressed. Many of her poems express that kindness. Others call up the quiet beauty of the South American landscape. Many reflect her love of children. Mistral's poetry radiates warmth and emotional power. In awarding the Nobel Prize, a member of the Swedish Academy called her the "spiritual queen of Latin America."

VOCABULARY

accurate (AK yuh ruht) *adj.* free from error; correct; exact
fiscal (FIS kuhl) *adj.* having to do with finances
compassionate (kuhm PASH en it) *adj.* deeply sympathetic

Roger D. Kornberg, Nobel Laureate in Chemistry

In 1959, Roger Kornberg saw his father, Arthur Kornberg, receive a Nobel Prize for his work with DNA. Roger was 12 years old. In 2006, Roger received his own Nobel Prize.

DNA is the carrier of genetic information. It's a blueprint that tells all the cells of the body what to do. DNA is stored inside the nucleus of our cells. To be used, however, the DNA's information must be copied onto RNA. RNA is the messenger. It carries the information out of the nucleus. The copy-process is called transcription.

Scientists had known about transcription for years. But they didn't know how it occurred. Roger Kornberg described *how* information is copied from DNA to RNA. For this work, he was awarded the Nobel Prize.

Hideki Yukawa, Nobel Laureate in Physics

In 1934, Hideki Yukawa predicted the existence of new particles called *mesons*. Mesons are tiny particles. They are heavier than electrons but lighter than protons. When experiments by other scientists proved him right, Yukawa set to work to **develop** his theory. In 1949, he was awarded the Nobel Prize in Physics for predicting a previously unknown particle.

World War II had just ended. In the award ceremony, the Academy called Yukawa "the very best example of the importance of science in bringing nations and races together." "Not many years ago," they added, "Japan and the United States stood against each other. . . . Today you work happily in the midst of American colleagues."

Just after World War II, Hideki Yukawa, a Japanese scientist, won the Nobel Prize in Physics. In 1948, Yukawa worked as a visiting professor at Princeton, and in 1949 at Columbia, both in the United States.

VOCABULARY

develop (di VEL uhp) *v.* grow or change into something bigger, stronger, or more advanced

Shared Nobel Laureates in Medicine

Sir Alexander Fleming became interested in bacteria during World War I. Many soldiers were dying not because of their injuries, but due to infection. After the war, he was working in his lab. A mold spore had drifted onto a Petri dish. The dish was filled with a culture of bacteria. As he was cleaning up, he noticed a bacteria-free circle around the mold. Fleming started doing experiments. Eventually, he proved that the mold prevented the growth of many kinds of bacteria. Fleming named the substance *penicillin.*

If Ernst B. Chain and Sir Howard Florey hadn't entered the scene, though, it might have been a long time before penicillin was widely used. To be used in humans, a purer form of penicillin was needed. Chain and Florey found a way to isolate the active substance. Thanks to their efforts, penicillin was available during World War II to treat war wounds. In 1945, all three men were honored for their work with penicillin.

The Nobel Peace Prize

According to Alfred Nobel the Peace Prize was to be awarded to someone who
- did the best work for fraternity between peoples,
- worked for the abolition or reduction of standing armies, and
- held and promoted peace congresses.

With these **criteria** in mind, the prize has been awarded for many things.

1964, Martin Luther King, Jr. In 1964, Martin Luther King, Jr. received the Nobel Peace Prize for working to **obtain** equal rights for African Americans. Mahatma Gandhi was one of King's heroes. Gandhi inspired many people in his nonviolent struggle for India's independence from Great Britain. Like Gandhi, King could not **justify** violence. He asked people to seek change

through nonviolent means. Using boycotts, sit-ins, and peaceful marches, thousands of people followed his lead. Refusing to fight back in the face of violence, the movement he began led to the U.S. Civil Rights Act of 1964. Among other things, it banned racial discrimination in public places.

In awarding the 1964 Peace Prize to Martin Luther King, Jr., the Nobel Committee said, "He is the first person in the Western world to have shown us that a struggle can be waged without violence."

VOCABULARY

criteria (kry TIR ee uh) *n.* standards or tests by which something can be judged

obtain (ubh TAYN) *v.* get something that you want, especially through your own effort, skill, or work

justify (JUS tuh fy) *v.* show to be just, right, or in accord with reason; validate

1989, The 14th Dalai Lama In 1989, the 14th Dalai Lama received the Nobel Peace Prize. It was given to him for his nonviolent campaign to end Chinese control of Tibet. The Dalai Lama believes that conflicts can be resolved by talking. However, that dialogue must reflect respect for others. Like King, the Dalai Lama sees himself as a successor to Mahatma Gandhi. Gandhi himself never received the award. In awarding the Peace Prize to the Dalai Lama, the Committee said that it should be regarded "as in part a tribute to the memory of Mahatma Gandhi."

2003, Shirin Ebadi Shirin Ebadi was the first woman from the Muslim world to receive the Nobel Peace Prize. As a lawyer, judge, and activist, she has spent her life speaking for the rights of women and children in her native Iran. In the face of threats to her own safety, she has always **supported** nonviolence as a means to change. Her bravery and self-sacrifice have made her a hero to many. In 2003, Ebadi was honored with the Nobel Peace Prize.

2003, Wangari Maathai Wangari Maathai was distributing food in a tiny African village when she learned she was the 2004 Peace Prize Laureate. To some people, the award seemed an odd choice. The award was being given to an environmentalist! In announcing the award, the Nobel Committee said, "Peace on earth depends on our ability to secure our living environment . . . She has taken a holistic approach to sustainable development that embraces democracy, human rights and women's rights."

In other words, everything is connected—peace, human rights, and the environment. When resources are scarce, wars begin. Maathai has rallied poor women and **assisted** them in planting 30 million trees. In the process, she has taught them about nutrition, family planning, and their rights. Her *goal* is to restore Africa's forests. Her *hope* is to end poverty and conflict caused by deforestation.

VOCABULARY

support (suh POHRT) *v.* provide evidence to prove or back up an idea

assist (uh SIST) *v.* give help to; make it easier for someone to do something

Wangari Maathai was the first environmentalist and the first African woman to win the Nobel Peace Prize.

Alfred Nobel's Family

Who was Alfred Nobel? What made him want to give millions of dollars to people he didn't know? And where did he get the money?

Alfred Nobel was the fourth son of Immanuel and Andrietta Nobel. He was born on October 21, 1833 in Stockholm, Sweden. Alfred's father was an inventor and engineer. Andrietta had eight children in a time when many children didn't live to adulthood. Four survived.

This portrait was taken when Alfred Nobel was 41 years old. By the age of 40, he was a wealthy man because of his invention of dynamite.

One, Emil, was born after Alfred. As was common in those days, all four boys went into their father's business, at least for a while.

Dad's business was not exactly safe or secure. He lost money, gained it back, and lost it again. He also moved around a lot. His most successful business was in St. Petersburg, Russia, where he manufactured explosives and other **devices** for the Russian Army. All of this interested his son Alfred.

Chemistry, Engineering, and Explosives

Immanuel's habit of moving rubbed off on Alfred. By age 16, Alfred was fluent in Swedish, English, French, German, and Russian. By 17, Alfred hoped to be a writer. His father, however, **implied** that writing was not a serious profession. So, in 1850, Alfred went to Paris to study chemistry. Then, he left for the United States. For four years, he assisted John Ericsson, a transplanted Swede and engineer. Ericsson later became famous for inventing the Union's Civil War battleship the *Monitor*.

Returning to Europe, Alfred worked in his father's St. Petersburg factory until it went bankrupt in 1859. Then, Alfred returned to Sweden.

Back in Sweden, Alfred experimented with explosives. He'd been interested in them since boyhood. Now, with the Industrial Revolution beginning, coal was

VOCABULARY

devices (di VYS uhz) *n.* techniques or means for working things out

implied (im PLYD) *v.* suggested

33

needed to power factories and steam trains. People used gunpowder to break through rock and get coal. The black powder, however, wasn't strong enough for really big explosions. Alfred wondered if he could manufacture something stronger.

New Explosives

Eventually, Alfred experimented with a new explosive called *nitroglycerin*. Nitroglycerin is an explosive yellow oil. It is made by adding glycerin to a mixture of nitric and sulfuric acid. Alfred started to manufacture it in 1862.

Nitroglycerin was an amazing new explosive, but it had drawbacks. It tended to explode without warning and without any apparent cause. Alfred was determined to find a safe way to transport it and safely detonate it. Nonetheless, many accidents happened. In 1864, his nitroglycerin factory blew up, killing his brother Emil and several other people. It was the first of many unplanned explosions around the world.

Eventually, Alfred found that he could combine nitroglycerin with *kieselguhr,* a crumbly kind of sandy earth, to make a safer, dry kind of explosive. He named the new explosive *dynamite.* The new explosive made Nobel's fortune.

Nobel's Daily Life

Alfred turned out to be a good businessman. He worked hard, often 15–18 hours a day. That didn't leave much time for a social life. However, along the way, he did meet a lifelong friend named Bertha von Suttner. He also wrote plays, novels, and poetry.

Bertha von Suttner was an author who became a leader in the peace movement. She devoted much of her time, energy, and writing to the cause of peace. She corresponded with people all over the world to promote peace projects.

Von Suttner was deeply concerned about war. She and Alfred must have had many conversations about where Alfred's money came from. Eventually, von Suttner became a pacifist. Nine years after Alfred's death, she won the Nobel Peace Prize.

In 1888, something happened that may have changed Alfred forever. His brother Ludvig died. On Ludvig's death, French papers carried this headline: "The Merchant of Death is Dead." They had confused Ludvig with Alfred. "Merchant of Death?" That wasn't what Alfred had set out to be. His explosives were mainly to be used in coal mining and construction. Yet they had become powerful forces in war.

Nobel's Legacy

Alfred died in Italy in 1896. When his will was opened, it astounded everyone. He'd left most of his fortune in trust to create the Nobel Prizes. Why? No one knows for sure.

The French headlines may have provided a powerful incentive. Add that to his lifelong **alliance** with von Suttner, and you have powerful motivators. Early in their friendship, von Suttner wrote a **pertinent** remark about her friend. Alfred, she wrote, wanted to make a device that would cause so much "devastation that it would make wars altogether impossible." It was a sentiment that came back in the 1960s and 70s as the concept of "mutually assured destruction." Alfred believed that if both sides of a conflict had weapons so terrible that they could utterly destroy the other side, there would be no point in fighting at all.

Alfred Nobel was full of contradictions. His inventions created massive destruction. Yet in his will, he established the world's most impressive prizes for offering service to humanity. Nobel was a poet himself. Most likely, he would have been delighted to hear poetry during Nobel ceremonies. Halldis Moren Vesaas wrote a beautiful poem that was read during the ceremony for Wangari Maathai. And, in Shirin Ebadi's ceremony, the Committee quoted many poets, including the great Persian poet, Saadi of Shiraz. In part, it reads: "He who is indifferent to the suffering of others is a traitor to that which is truly human."

VOCABULARY

alliance (uh LY uhns) *n.* people united for a common goal

pertinent (PERT uhn uhnt) *adj.* relevant; having a connection

This photo shows the Nobel Diploma and gold medal awarded to South Korean President Kim Dae-Jung during the 2000 Nobel Peace Prize ceremony.

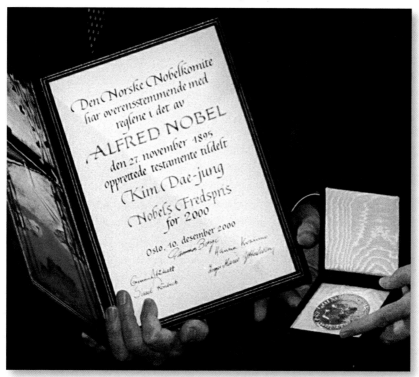

And the Nobel Prize Goes to . . .

Nobel Prizes usually go to one person. They can also be split between two or three people. The Peace Prize has been given to several organizations. The International Committee of the Red Cross has won the Nobel Peace Prize three times: in 1917, 1944, and 1963. One man, Linus Pauling, has won unshared Nobel Prizes in two categories: Chemistry and Peace. The youngest person to win a Nobel Prize was 25 years old. Lawrence Bragg won for Physics.

You have probably heard of more Nobel Laureates. Which ones **challenge** you to do your best in *your* field of interest?

Conclusion

Nobel Prizes have been awarded to men and women from many different countries. Most have gone to people who have **devoted** their lives to their efforts. They have **invested** their hard work, talents, imaginations, and hearts to their endeavors.

Some, like Mother Teresa, have given out of deep **compassion** for the suffering of the poor. Others, like James Watson, Francis Crick, and Maurice Wilkins, have **responded** to life with a deep commitment to uncovering its mysteries. Writers, like Toni Morrison, have used their talents to bring the history or experiences of their people to life. Still others, like Riccardo Giacconi, Masatoshi

Koshiba, and Raymond Davis, Jr., **focused** their curiosity on the makeup of the universe and made surprising **discoveries**. Each in a different way has helped us learn about our world.

Alfred Nobel's final wish was to honor people who have made noble contributions to life on this planet. The Nobel Prizes help us to honor and remember these very special people.

Discussion Questions

1. What is the importance of the Nobel Prizes?

2. Of all the people who have received a Nobel Prize, who deserves it the most?

3. How do you explain the contradictions in Alfred Nobel? What do you think of him?

VOCABULARY

challenge (CHAL uhnj) *v.* call to take part in a contest or competition

devote (di VOHT) *v.* set apart for a special use or service; dedicate

invest (in VEST) *v.* spend time or effort with the expectation of some satisfaction

compassion (kuhm PASH uhn) *n.* sympathy for others who are suffering, along with the urge to help them

respond (ri SPAHND) *v.* react to something that has been said or done

focus (FOH kuhs) *v.* concentrate on one thing

discovery (di SKUV er ee) *n.* the revealing of something or someone that was hidden or unknown before

STAMPS: TINY WINDOWS ON THE WORLD

The world sends you messages every day, but how many do you recognize? A newspaper tells you what's happening, but only if you read it. Advertisements reveal not only what's for sale, but also trends and fashions. Some of the messages are so small, you might not even notice them. Look in the upper-right corner of any envelope. You're likely to find a small square or rectangular stamp. It might seem like something **trivial**, a useful product and nothing more. Take a closer look and you'll see that stamps tell a great deal about the world, its past, and its people.

Many people collect stamps from around the world.

caption tk

Stamps are more than postage. The images on stamps present portraits of our world. Countries around the world use stamps to celebrate the contributions of fascinating people; acknowledge geographic marvels; and commemorate key events in history.

Don't let the size of stamps fool you. They can **communicate** messages just as powerfully as a giant billboard. In fact, stamps have something that most posters do not: government approval. The fact that a government has decided to honor the subject of a stamp **suggests** that it might really be worthy of your attention.

Stamps **appeal** to many people because of their colorful images. When you take the time to look at them, you'll begin to **appreciate** these tiny artworks. They can take you on surprising journeys as you **explore** the **topics** they honor.

VOCABULARY

trivial (TRIV ee uhl) *adj.* of little importance

communicate (kuh MYOO ni kayt) *v.* express your thoughts and feelings clearly, so that other people understand them

suggest (suhg JEST) *v.* show indirectly; imply

appeal (uh PEEL) *v.* be attractive or interesting; arouse a favorable response

appreciate (uh PREE shee ayt) *v.* recognize and be grateful for; think well of; understand and enjoy

explore (ek SPLOHR) *v.* examine a place or thing closely to learn more about it

topic (TAHP ik) *n.* the subject

How Stamps Got Started

Stamps did not exist before 1840. Until then, people paid for mail when they received it. The amount of postage was based on the distance the letter had traveled. An Englishman named Rowland Hill noticed several problems with this system. People often refused to accept letters, so they had to be returned and the shipper received no money at all. Hill also figured out that the most expensive part of delivering mail is sorting the letters. Carrying them is not as expensive.

Hill suggested a simple but important reform. He suggested that all postage should be prepaid by the sender, who would pay a fixed rate regardless of how far the letter was going. The first postage stamp appeared on May 1, 1840. It showed Queen Victoria. The stamps were printed on plain paper, so buyers had to cut them apart with scissors. About eight years later, Britain began printing stamps edged with tiny perforations, or holes that make them easy to separate.

Other countries saw that Hill's postal reform made a lot of sense. In 1847, the United States issued its first stamps: a 5-cent stamp showing Benjamin Franklin and a 10-cent stamp showing George Washington. Stamps were soon being issued in Austria, Germany, and throughout the world.

Commemorative Editions The Australian colony of New South Wales changed stamp history in 1888. The government printed a stamp honoring the 100th anniversary of the founding of the colony. This was the first

These commemorative stamps depict historical transportation.

commemorative postage stamp. Commemorative stamps are special because they are printed only once. As a result, they are limited editions. When the first printing is sold, they are no longer available.

Countries use commemorative stamps to honor important events, people, or subjects. Stamps ensure that **posterity** will remember the important contributions of its special citizens. They also present an **eloquent history** of a country's values. Let's look at some famous firsts in U.S. stamps. They will **illustrate** how the world of honorees expanded greatly in the 20th century.

VOCABULARY

posterity (pahs TER uh tee) *n.* future generations; descendants

eloquent (EL uh kwuhnt) *adj.* vividly expressive

history (HIS tuh ree) *n.* an account of things that happened in the past

illustrate (IL uh strayt) *v.* make the meaning of something clearer by giving examples

The First Women on U.S. Stamps

USA 15¢

HELEN KELLER
ANNE SULLIVAN

This stamp honored Helen Keller and her teacher Anne Sullivan. Although blind and deaf, Helen Keller overcame these disabilities to become a noted author and lecturer.

It was almost 50 years before the United States Postal Service issued a stamp that showed a woman. You might be surprised to learn that she wasn't from the United States. In 1893, the government issued a series of 15 stamps honoring Christopher Columbus. Queen Isabella of Spain, the sponsor of Columbus's expedition to North America, was depicted on four of these stamps.

The first U.S. woman to show up on a stamp was former first-lady Martha Washington in 1902. The next women portrayed subjects rather than specific women. A girl posed near a tree to honor Arbor Day in 1932. Two years later, artist James Whistler's famous portrait of his own mother appeared on a stamp. However, this stamp was not issued to pay tribute to Whistler's mother herself. The text **cites** the stamp's more general **focus**. It reads: "in memory and honor of the mothers of America."

In 1936, Susan B. Anthony gained her place in stamp history. Anthony **devoted** her passionate energy to helping women gain the right to vote.

Famous Americans Series As you can see, very few women were portrayed in the first 90 years of U.S. stamps. Why? The answer is that most stamps focused on political history, and women had been prevented from entering politics. In 1940, the Postal Service expanded its focus with a landmark series called *Famous Americans.* This series **emphasized** the contributions of 35 U.S. citizens in seven categories: authors, poets, educators, scientists, composers, artists, and inventors. The series included two prominent women.

Louisa Mae Alcott, who wrote *Little Women,* was one of the authors **selected** for this series. Jane Addams was one of the scientists. Addams worked in the social sciences. She founded Hull House, a landmark settlement house providing housing and education to Chicago's poor.

VOCABULARY

cite (SYT) *v.* refer to an example or fact as proof

focus (FOH kuhs) *n.* the central point of a work

devote (di VOHT) *v.* set apart for a special use or service; dedicate

emphasize (EM fuh syz) *v.* show that an opinion, idea, or quality is especially important; say a word or phrase louder or higher than others to give it more importance

select (suh LEKT) *v.* choose something or someone by carefully thinking about which is the best or most appropriate

Stamps Begin to Honor African Americans

Like women, African Americans were prevented from playing active roles in politics and government. As a result, none appeared on postage stamps until the *Famous Americans* series appeared in 1940. One of the educators featured was Booker T. Washington. Born into slavery but freed by emancipation in 1863, Washington founded one of the first universities for African Americans. To build the school that would become Tuskegee University, Washington had to overcome fierce racial **bias** and unashamed **ignorance**.

Black Heritage Series Launched in 1978, the Black Heritage stamp series celebrates African American men and women who have **contributed** to U.S. life and culture. The first stamp in this series was also the first U.S. stamp to show an African American woman. Harriet Tubman escaped slavery, but then returned to Maryland to help her sister and two children escape to freedom. Tubman became one of the leading abolitionists before the Civil War. She helped more than 300 slaves find freedom by following the Underground Railroad to Canada.

Since the series began, Black Heritage has honored a wide variety of African Americans in many fields:

- **Government and Civil Rights:** Martin Luther King, Jr., Whitney Moore Young, A. Philip Randolph, Ida B. Wells, Malcolm X, Patricia Harris, Roy Wilkins, Thurgood Marshall.

These ten stamps commemorating jazz musicians were unveiled at a 1995 jazz festival.

- **Science and Invention:** Benjamin Banneker, Jan Ernst Matzeliger, Percy Lavon Julian, Ernest E. Just, Madam C.J. Walker.
- **Sports and Recreation:** Jackie Robinson, Bessie Coleman.
- **Fine Arts:** Scott Joplin, James P. Johnson, W.E.B. DuBois, Langston Hughes, Paul Robeson, Ella Fitzgerald.
- **Education:** Carter G. Woodson, Mary McLeod Bethune, Allison Davis.
- **Exploration:** Jean Baptiste Pointe Du Sable.

Look up any of these names in an encyclopedia or the Internet to find out about the life of a great U.S. citizen.

VOCABULARY

bias (BY uhs) *n.* unfair preference or dislike for someone or something

ignorance (IG nuh ruhns) *n.* lack of knowledge or awareness

contribute (kuhn TRIB yoot) *v.* give money, help, or ideas to something that other people are also involved in

47

Acknowledging Fine Artists

U.S. stamp history began with George Washington and Benjamin Franklin. But after the landmark *Famous Americans* series, stamps began to acknowledge public figures who were not politicians. Since 1940, the **criteria** for being put on a postage stamp has expanded. Stamps now honor people in many different fields.

The stamp bearing the image of Georgia O'Keeffe's famous red poppy was released in April, 1996.

Writers The Postal Service has issued dozens of stamps honoring well-known writers. John Steinbeck, Willa Cather, F. Scott Fitzgerald, Tennessee Williams, Edith Wharton, and Zora Neale Hurston have all appeared on letters sent around the world. In 2004, beloved children's author Theodor Geisel received a stamp. You might know him better by his pen name, Dr. Seuss.

Musicians Stamps have celebrated composers **involved** in creating a huge variety of American music. Crowds at parades today still appreciate John Philip Sousa's brassy marches. Scott Joplin's ragtime music brought exciting new rhythms to music in the United States. Those rhythms were further stretched and developed by jazz artists such as Duke Ellington, Charlie Parker, and Billie Holiday.

The Broadway musical is another art form born in the United States. Stamps have featured well-known music and lyrics teams like Rodgers and Hammerstein, Lerner and Loewe, and the Gershwin brothers.

Popular singers like Al Jolson and Ethel Merman have their own stamps. And country singers honored have included Hank Williams and Patsy Cline. But Elvis Presley is still the King. His stamp is the most collected commemorative, with more than 124 million sold.

Artists People who have created memorable paintings and sculptures are commemorated, too. Frederick Remington was honored in both 1940 and again in 1961 and 1981 for his memorable artworks of the West. One of Frida Kahlo's striking self-portraits was placed on a stamp in 2001. A bright red poppy presented one of Georgia O'Keeffe's eloquent symbols. Other artists honored include John James Audobon, Mary Cassatt, and Andy Warhol.

VOCABULARY

criteria (kry TIR ee uh) *n.* standards or tests by which something can be judged

involve (in VAHLV) *v.* include something as a necessary part or result

Media Personalities The world of entertainment has **captured** people's interest since the earliest days of theater and radio. U.S. stamps have honored celebrities known for plays, movies, films, and television programs. The first person from the world of Hollywood was Walt Disney in 1968. He was surrounded by some of his own cartoon friends. The director D.W. Griffith received a stamp in 1975. Later stamps celebrated popular movie stars from silent film actors like Charlie Chaplin and Clara Bow to screen legends like Marilyn Monroe, John Wayne, Audrey Hepburn, and James Dean.

Television has played a key role in entertainment history. Stamps have honored comic stars like Lucille Ball, Jack Benny, and Milton Berle. One stamp paid tribute to the newscaster Edward R. Murrow.

Sports Stamps

Athletes have also received growing attention from the U.S. Postal Service. Many sports stamps acknowledge the important role that these sports play in our lives, rather than honoring specific athletes.

In 1932, a series of stamps honored the Olympic Games. Baseball was honored for the first time on a stamp in 1939.

In 1961, Dr. James Naismith was the focus of a commemorative stamp. You may not know his name, but chances are good you know the game he created. Back in 1891, he decided to create a new indoor game. Basketball has been popular ever since.

Stamps have focused on extreme sports, including skateboarding, inline skating, snowboarding, and BMX biking. Duke Kahanamoku, one of surfing's greats, received his own stamp in 2002.

These sports stamps honor Jesse Owens, who won four track events at the 1936 Olympics, and Jackie Robinson, who was the first African American to play in the major leagues.

capture (KAP chuhr) *v.* succeed in showing or describing a situation or feeling using words or pictures, so that other people can see, understand, or experience it

51

So Who Gets to Be on a Stamp, Anyway?

The U.S. Postal Service points out that stamps portray "the American experience to a world audience." Each year, they decide on about 25 people, events, and topics to honor with postage stamps. Many of the ideas come from people like you. Anyone can suggest a theme for a stamp. However, there are some rules you have to follow:

- Themes are primarily American or related to America.
- No one living can be shown on a stamp. Subjects must have been dead for five years. U.S. presidents are the only exception to this rule. They may be honored one year after their death.
- Historical events will be commemorated on anniversaries in multiples of 50 years.
- Events should be of national significance.
- A stamp cannot honor a specific city, primary or secondary school, hospital, library, or similar institution. There are too many of these in the United States to single only a few out for commemoration.
- Colleges can be honored, but only on the 200th anniversary of their founding.
- Acknowledging the separation of church and state, stamps will not honor specific religious institutions or leaders. Holidays, such as Christmas, Hanukkah, and Kwanzaa, are allowed.
- Stamp themes can only be repeated after 50 years have passed. Holidays and national symbols are exempt from this rule.

Sydney Chaplin stands next to an enlarged stamp featuring his father, Charlie Chaplin, in his most famous silent-film role as the "Little Tramp."

If you have a great idea for a stamp, send it here:

> Citizens' Stamp Advisory Committee
> c/o Stamp Development
> U.S. Postal Service
> 1735 North Lynn St., Suite 5013
> Arlington, VA 22209-6432

Remember, the stamp approval process takes time. So if you're suggesting an event, make sure the commemorative date is at least three years away.

Now You Don't Have to Be Dead to Be on a Stamp!

The rules for commemorative stamps are very strict. But thanks to exciting new technology, you don't need to wait until five years after you're dead to be on a stamp. Anyone can put their own photos on a genuine postage stamp. You could even mail the family dog around the world!

Custom-made stamps have become very popular for invitations and holiday mailings. Using computer software and the Internet, you can upload a digital photograph. A few clicks later, your order is complete. Soon, your mail carrier will bring you a sheet of postage stamps with your own photograph.

The key difference between your stamps and the Elvis stamp is that yours are not commemorative stamps. They are personal stamps. The Postal Service can **maintain** their strict rules and still allow people to express themselves with stamps.

Of course, there are still a few rules that you have to follow. You must own the rights to the photo you use. You cannot include pictures of celebrities. Offensive pictures are not allowed. Visit the website for more rules and complete instructions.

Collecting Stamps and Stories

Every stamp tells a story. Many people around the world enjoy collecting these tiny stories. Their collections let them explore the world and history. A stamp collection can satisfy your **curiosity** to know more about the

These foreign stamps show colorful butterflies.

world. Looking at stamps might even **motivate** you to plan an actual journey.

Collections can be organized many ways. Some collectors specialize in stamps from one country. Others focus on a theme, such as Hollywood, butterflies, or World War II. The condition of a stamp is key. Unused stamps are the most valuable. Perfect stamps are **defined** as "in mint condition." Collectors use special envelopes and albums to maintain the condition of their stamps.

Vocabulary

maintain (mayn TAYN) *v.* make something continue in the same way or at the same standard as before

curiosity (kyoor ee AHS uh tee) *n.* desire to learn about or know something

motivate (MOH tuh vayt) *v.* make someone want to achieve something and make them willing to work hard in order to do it

define (dee FYN) *v.* state the meaning

The Value of Stamps The most valuable stamps are the rarest. Some stamps are rare because very few were printed. Others are valuable because of mistakes. If the printing on a stamp is not **accurate**, its value can go sky high.

One of the most famous stamp errors is the 1918 Inverted Jenny. Due to a printing error, the biplane on the stamp was printed upside-down. A rare four-block set of these stamps sold recently for $2.94 million.

Luckily, you don't need to be a millionaire to start collecting stamps. Many stamps are very reasonably priced. And the appeal of stamps is greater than their value in dollars. Stamps are tiny windows that open into an eloquent world of images and ideas.

A forgery, on the left, of the rare Inverted Jenny stamp is held next to an original, on the right.

Discussion Questions

1. What can you learn about a country by studying its stamps? What can't you learn from this source?

2. What does the history of U.S. stamps tell the world about our country?

3. How do stamps communicate messages about a country's values and ideals? Choose one or two specific stamps and explain what message is being sent whenever the stamp is used.

4. What subject would you recommend for a commemorative stamp? Why?

5. Anyone other than a U.S. president must have been dead for at least five years before appearing on a U.S. postage stamp. Why do you think this rule was made? Do you think it is necessary? Why or why not?

Vocabulary

accurate (AK yuh ruht) *adj.* free from error; correct; exact

THE GROWTH OF THE INTERNET

You know about the Internet, that huge entity out there in cyberspace that has changed the world.

But just what *is* the Internet and how big is it anyway? Okay, those may not seem like burning questions. But in today's world of instant messaging and online marketing, the answers are probably good to know. So here we go.

The Internet (or "The Net," for short) is a global network of connected computers created by ARPA. The Internet allows people to share and find information by accessing websites and other computer users. Since its beginning in the 60s, the Net has grown exponentially to encompass the entire world.

"Wait, wait, wait!" you say. "ARPA? Global network? Exponentially? What does all that mean?"

We're glad you asked.

A "Net" Is Born

The Internet was born in the 1960s, and like most new-borns, it started off really small. There was no such thing as global emailing or a gazillion websites hanging out in cyberspace. All of that fun stuff was yet to come. The Internet **originated** as a modest research project carried out by the Department of Defense.

One of its agencies, called the Advanced Research Projects Agency or ARPA, thought it would be a good idea to connect computers so that information on one computer could be sent to other computers. So, the agency began to **investigate** ways to build networks of computers. In 1969 four computers were connected to form a network called ARPANET. (ARPA-NET. Get it?) This little network was, in fact, a baby Internet. However, the ARPA scientists had bigger **aspirations**.

Two students access the Internet wirelessly in Los Angeles.

VOCABULARY

originate (uh RIJ i NAYT) *v.* begin or develop from a particular place or situation

investigate (in VES tuh gayt) *v.* search into so as to learn the facts

aspirations (as puh RAY shunz) *n.* strong desires or ambitions

Bringing Up the Net

During the 1970s and 1980s, other networks were created, but they **involved** only a few computers each. Just a handful of people used them, mainly computer scientists working for governments or for universities.

The 70s and 80s was a time of great innovation. In the 1970s, scientists developed the first electronic mail, or what we now call email. (On March 26, 1976, Queen Elizabeth II of England visited the Royal Signals and Radar Establishment, and sent her first email.)

Researchers also developed computer protocols, a fancy word for *ways to do something.* These protocols established standardized ways for computers to send information to other computers. Once the protocols were wired into the system, they **enabled** small networks to link up to each other, creating larger **harmonious** networks.

Linking up networks is known as "inter-networking." That's where the term "Internet" comes from. The Internet

Leonard Kleinrock, a computer scientist at UCLA, stands next to the refrigerator-sized computer that made the first connection in 1969 to what would become the Internet.

is a network of networks. Just as networks consist of computers joined up to share information, the Internet consists of many smaller networks joined together.

The Net Neighborhood

It was also during these early days of the Internet that computer scientists developed the system of domain names. (*Domain* means *a particular area of influence*.) Domains are the areas in which the hosts exist, i.e., government, commercial, education, and so on.

Hosts are the computers that actually contain the information you find on the Internet. Hosts send email between computers. Hosts also maintain websites. So when you access a website online, you are connecting to a distant host computer that sends the information on its website back to your computer.

In the 1970s, when domain names were given to collective hosts, websites hadn't been invented yet. Domain names were **devoted** to locating and connecting hosts and downloading information. When websites were developed, domain names became part of the "www" addresses we now use to find a website, for example, ".gov," ".com," and ".edu."

VOCABULARY

involve (in VAHLV) *v.* include something as a necessary part or result

enable (en AY buhl) *v.* give someone what they need to be able to do something

harmonious (hahr MOH nee uhs) *adj.* combined in a pleasing, orderly arrangement

devote (di VOHT) *v.* set apart for a special use or service; dedicate

The Internet Grows Up

In the late 1980s, the government, who up to then had restricted use of the Internet to the military and scientists, opened the Internet to the public. Internet service providers, which serve as relay stations between hosts, sold their services to private computer owners. Here's the cool part. The service providers allowed any computer network to connect: the very large, the very small, the very fast, and the very slow. Now people within any network could **obtain** information on computers in other networks. It was an "open" system, meaning every computer user was allowed to **benefit** from the new technology.

Suddenly everyone who signed on with a service provider could connect or *get online*. Almost as suddenly, millions of people began **participating** in online activities. The number of website hosts within different domains increased. Commercial enterprises, news affiliations, educational institutions, and special interest groups for every known **topic** established websites that informed, entertained, and sold products.

People responded enthusiastically. They used the Internet increasingly to find books, articles, entertainment, news, maps and directions, and even deals on products and services. And, of course, the Internet allowed a quick, easy way to **communicate** with friends and family through email. The world was literally at our fingertips!

This 1996 photo shows a high-school student connecting
to the Internet with the help of a teacher.

Vocabulary

obtain (uhb TAYN) *v.* get something that you want, especially
through your own effort, skill, or work

benefit (BEN uh fit) *v.* bring advantages to someone or improve
their lives in some way

participate (pahr TIS uh payt) *v.* take part in an activity or event

topic (TAHP ik) *n.* the subject

communicate (kuh MYOO ni kayt) *v.* express your thoughts and
feelings clearly, so that other people understand them

Google is one way to search the World Wide Web.

The World Wide Web

The rapid growth of the Internet in the 1990s was the result of another technological breakthrough: the browser (as in *browse,* which means to look around for something in a leisurely manner). It's an apt name, because an online browser is a program that **assists** users in their search for websites over the Internet. The first online browser, created in 1990, was the only way to visit the Web. It was called WorldWideWeb. Later the program name was changed to Nexus. The abstract space where websites reside was renamed World Wide Web, with spaces between the words.

Websites quickly became interactive, offering many online options. Today, users can go to a website and find a menu of links (connections). With a "point and click" of a mouse, a user can access additional images, music, services, and other related sites. This is a giant leap from simply transferring data between computers. So the World Wide Web (often referred to as "The Web") grew rapidly. At the beginning of 1993 there were just 130 websites online. Three years later there were 230,000, and the number continued to grow.

Sometimes people use the terms "Web" and "Internet" as if they were the same. It's important to **emphasize** the difference between them. The Internet is the global network of computers connected by Internet service providers. It is used to send email or transfer files. The Internet is made from real stuff: computers and cables. The Web is an intangible space. It refers to all the websites that **pervade** the Internet, but it has no material qualities. It exists within the programs that communicate between computers on the Net.

Vocabulary

assist (uh SIST) *v.* give help to; make it easier for someone to do something

emphasize (EM fuh syz) *v.* show that an opinion, idea, or quality is especially important; say a word or phrase louder or higher than others to give it more importance

pervade (puhr VAYD) *v.* spread throughout

Growth of the Net

The Web could not exist without the Net. This does not **imply** that the Web is less important. Quite the contrary. It's the Web that makes the Net so useful for so many. People who aren't at all interested in computers and cables are very interested in the **diverting** possibilities websites have to offer. The growing number of websites **contributes** to the Net's growth, and the Net has grown phenomenally since the late 1980s.

By 1992, just a few years after the Internet opened to the general public, over 4 million people were going online. The Internet encompassed more than 700,000 host computers in over 5,000 computer networks.

Figure 1 graphically **illustrates** the number of hosts on the Internet each year from 1994 to 2006. The

Figure 1

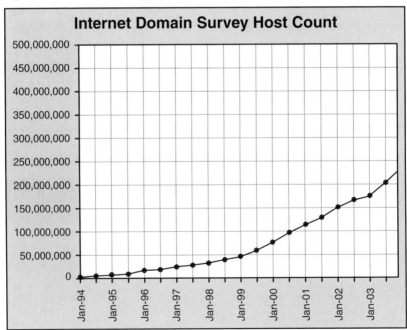

curved line shows how the number has grown very large very quickly.

Table 1 **captures** the yearly number of host computers online plus the ratio to the previous year. These **statistics** show that at the beginning of 1993 there were a little over a million Internet hosts. By the beginning of 1996, there were nearly 10 million hosts.

Table 1

Month/Year	# of Websites	Ratio to previous year
January 1993	1,300,000	——
January 1994	2,200,000	1.69
January 1995	4,900,000	2.23
January 1996	9,500,000	1.94

Each year there are many more host computers on the Internet than the year before. In fact, every year, the number of Internet hosts roughly doubled, as the middle column shows.

VOCABULARY

imply (im PLY) *v.* hint at; suggest

diverting (duh VERT ing) *adj.* distracting; amusing

contribute (kuhn TRIB yoot) *v.* give money, help, or ideas to something that other people are also involved in

illustrate (IL uh strayt) *v.* make the meaning of something clearer by giving examples

capture (KAP chuhr) *v.* succeed in showing or describing a situation or feeling using words or pictures, so that other people can see, understand, or experience it

statistics (stuh TIS tiks) *n.* collection of numbers or data that represent facts or measurements

It's not just the number of hosts online that's growing. The number of *new* hosts added every year is growing, too. The right-hand column in **Table 2** shows the number of new hosts added each year between 1993 and 1996.

Table 2

Year	Hosts	New hosts
1993	1,300,000	——
1994	2,200,000	900,000
1995	4,900,000	2,700,000
1996	9,500,000	4,600,000

Exponential Growth What these figures show is that the Internet is growing exponentially every year. Now, here's how we **define** exponential growth—and hey, this is a good thing to know. Something grows exponentially when it is multiplied by a fixed amount every turn of a fixed cycle. Let's look at an easy example. Do you know that game in which every correct answer earns you double the amount of points you earned for the answer before? Let's say the first answer wins 25 points. Then the second correct answer earns 50 points. The third answer, 100 points, and so on. If you're really smart, you can earn 1,000,000 points after 15 turns. That's exponential growth.

Here's another example. If you put money in a bank it earns interest. Every year the money increases by a certain multiple, that's the *interest rate*. With an interest rate of 5% a year, your money multiplies by 1.05 every year. That might not seem like much, but remember, by increasing the full amount of every year's growth by 5%, it eventually adds up to quite a lot.

Accelerated Growth Getting back to the Internet. Because the Internet is growing exponentially, its *speed of growth* is accelerating as well. Like an accelerating car, it started off slowly, then it grew faster, and then faster still.

Look back at **Figure 1**, the graph of Internet hosts. As you go from left to right (from earlier in time to later) the graph curves upward. Why does it curve? Thinking in terms of an accelerating car may help to explain why the graph shows a curve rather then a straight line.

VOCABULARY

define (dee FYN) *v.* state the meaning

These race cars are accelerating during the 2004 Spanish Grand Prix.

Figure 2

**Ratio of Distance to Speed
in an Accelerating Car**

Accelerating
Constant Speed

Distance (feet)

Time (seconds)

Look at **Figure 2**, which illustrates the distance covered by an accelerating car and a car that isn't accelerating. A car going at a constant speed (not accelerating) covers the same distance every second. Imagine a car driving at 60 miles per hour (mph). It covers 88 feet every second. The red line shows how much distance the car has covered at each point in time. The line shows a constant slope ("rise over run") because the distance the car has gone increases by the same amount every second.

But a car that is accelerating *goes faster each second* than it did the second before. So in each second, it covers more distance than it did in the last second. The blue line is the graph of the distance that an accelerating car covers in a given amount of time. It curves upwards. The slope of the graph for the accelerating car gets steeper and steeper over time, as the car covers a greater distance each second.

So, what would **Figure 1** (Internet hosts) tell you if the graph showing the host count were moving in a straight line? You got it.

The Net and Exponential Equations

You may have noticed that the number of hosts online doesn't *exactly* double every year. As you can see in **Table 1,** sometimes the ratio of hosts in one year to the number of hosts the previous year is a little more than 2, sometimes a little less. The real world usually doesn't fit mathematical equations precisely. But we can use mathematical equations to describe the world *approximately* and understand it better. The growth of the Internet is *approximately* equal to an exponential equation. If we wanted to estimate the size of the Internet five years from now, using an exponential equation would be a good way to do it.

Let's consider an example of an equation that describes the growth of the Net. Suppose the number of hosts doubles every year. If there are 1,300,000 hosts in year *0*, then there are $1{,}300{,}000 \times 2 = 2{,}600{,}000$ hosts in year *1*.

In year *2*, there are $2{,}600{,}000 \times 2 = 5{,}200{,}000$ hosts. In other words, there are $1{,}300{,}000 \times 2 \times 2$ hosts in year *2*. A simple way to write this is $1{,}300{,}000(2^2)$.

In year *3* there are $1{,}300{,}000(2^3) = 10{,}400{,}000$ hosts.

Do you see a pattern emerging? The number of hosts in any year *t* equals: $1{,}300{,}000(2^t)$. It's really just the old "double the points" game described earlier.

Figure 3

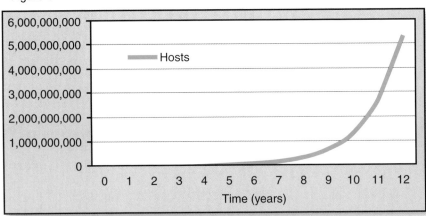

This graph shows the approximate growth of the Net.

Figure 3 is a graphical representation of the formula 1,300,000(2^t), our approximation of the growth of the Net. Note how similar the shape of the graph is to the graph in **Figure 1**.

Growing Beyond Tomorrow

More people are becoming Internet users and creating new websites every day. That means more people are sharing more information with a wider audience. As a result, traffic on the information highway is becoming crowded. If the Internet is to continue to grow, Internet capacity must increase to accommodate the increased traffic. Luckily, researchers are constantly developing new technologies that increase the speed, capacity, and **utility** of the Net.

So how will this bigger, faster, more efficient Internet affect your world? Think about it: an ever-expanding universe of knowledge, ideas, and services, right at your fingertips—anytime, anywhere.

Discussion Questions

1. How has the Internet benefited you? How do you imagine the Internet will serve you in the future?

2. What does it mean to say that the real world doesn't always "fit" mathematical equations precisely? Why is it useful to use equations to understand the world anyway?

3. Imagine two small countries, Alpha and Beta, that both have a population of 1 million this year. The population of Alpha increases by 1% each year. The population of Beta increases by 20,000 people every year. Which country will have a bigger population next year? Will that country always have a bigger population? Why or why not?

VOCABULARY

utility (yoo TIL uh tee) *n.* the quality or property of being useful

Glossary

accurate (AK yuh ruht) *adj.* free from error; correct; exact **5, 24, 56**

alliance (uh LY uhns) *n.* people united for a common goal **36**

appeal (uh PEEL) *v.* be attractive or interesting; arouse a favorable response **41**

appreciate (uh PREE shee ayt) *v.* recognize and be grateful for; think well of; understand and enjoy **11, 41**

aspirations (as puh RAY shunz) *n.* strong desires or ambitions **59**

assist (uh SIST) *v.* give help to; make it easier for someone to do something **7, 31, 64**

benefit (BEN uh fit) *v.* bring advantages to someone or improve their lives in some way **23, 62**

bias (BY uhs) *n.* unfair preference or dislike for someone or something **46**

capture (KAP chuhr) *v.* succeed in showing or describing a situation or feeling using words or pictures, so that other people can see, understand, or experience it **7, 50, 67**

challenge (CHAL uhnj) *n.* something that tests strength, skill, or ability; an invitation to someone to try to defeat you in a game or a fight **5**

challenge (CHAL uhnj) *v.* call to take part in a contest or competition **38**

cite (SYT) *v.* refer to an example or fact as proof **44**

communicate (kuh MYOO ni kayt) *v.* express your thoughts and feelings clearly, so that other people understand them **41, 62**

compassion (kuhm PASH uhn) *n.* sympathy for others who are suffering, along with the urge to help them **38**

compassionate (kuhm PASH en it) *adj.* deeply sympathetic **25**

contribute (kuhn TRIB yoot) *v.* give money, help, or ideas to something that other people are also involved in **23, 46, 66**

credible (KRED uh buhl) *adj.* believable; reliable **11**

criteria (kry TIR ee uh) *n.* standards or tests by which something can be judged **11, 28, 48**

curiosity (kyoor ee AHS uh tee) *n.* desire to learn about or know something **54**

define (dee FYN) *v.* state the meaning **55, 68**

develop (di VEL uhp) *v.* grow or change into something bigger, stronger, or more advanced **26**

devices (di VYS uhz) *n.* techniques or means for working things out **13, 33**

devote (di VOHT) *v.* set apart for a special use or service; dedicate **5, 38, 45, 61**

discovery (di SKUV er ee) *n.* the revealing of something or someone that was hidden or unknown before **39**

disheveled (di SHEV uld) *adj.* untidy; rumpled **14**

diverting (duh VERT ing) *adj.* distracting; amusing **66**

eloquent (EL uh kwuhnt) *adj.* vividly expressive **43**

emphasize (EM fuh syz) *v.* show that an opinion, idea, or quality is especially important; say a word or phrase louder or higher than others to give it more importance **45, 65**

enable (en AY buhl) *v.* give someone what they need to be able to do something **8, 23, 60**

evidence (EV uh duhns) *n.* facts, objects, or signs that make you believe something exists or is true **8**

explore (ek SPLOHR) *v.* examine a place or thing closely to learn more about it **41**

fastidious (fa STID ee uhs) *adj.* not easy to please; very critical of anything crude or coarse **10**

fiscal (FIS kuhl) *adj.* having to do with finances **25**

focus (FOH kuhs) *n.* the central point of a work **13, 44**

focus (FOH kuhs) *v.* concentrate on one thing **39**

history (HIS tuh ree) *n.* an account of things that happened in the past **43**

ignorance (IG nuh ruhns) *n.* lack of knowledge or awareness **16, 46**

illustrate (IL uh strayt) *v.* make the meaning of something clearer by giving examples **13, 43, 66**

implied (im PLYD) *v.* suggested **11, 33**

imply (im PLY) *v.* hint at; suggest **66**

impress (im PRES) *v.* have a marked effect on the mind or emotions of someone **9**

incentive (in SENT iv) *n.* something that makes a person act **23**

infuse (in FYOOZ) *v.* put into **13**

invest (in VEST) *v.* spend time or effort with the expectation of some satisfaction **38**

investigate (in VES tuh gayt) *v.* search into so as to learn the facts **9, 59**

involve (in VAHLV) *v.* include something as a necessary part or result **48, 60**

justify (JUS tuh fy) *v.* show to be just, right, or in accord with reason; validate **29**

maintain (mayn TAYN) *v.* make something continue in the same way or at the same standard as before **54**

minimize (MIN uh myz) *v.* make the degree or amount of something as small as possible **23**

motivate (MOH tuh vayt) *v.* make someone want to achieve something and make them willing to work hard in order to do it **55**

obtain (uhb TAYN) *v.* get something that you want, especially through your own effort, skill, or work **7, 29, 62**

originate (uh RIJ i NAYT) *v.* begin or develop from a particular place or situation **59**

participate (pahr TIS uh payt) *v.* take part in an activity or event **10, 62**

pertinent (PERT uhn uhnt) *adj.* relevant; having a connection **36**

pervade (puhr VAYD) *v.* spread throughout **65**

posterity (pahs TER uh tee) *n.* future generations; descendants **43**

preservation (PREZ er VAY shuhn) *n.* the act of keeping something unchanged or unharmed **15**

rely (ree LY) *v.* trust someone or something to do what you need or expect them to do **9**

research (REE serch) *n.* careful, systematic study or investigation of a topic or field of knowledge **7**

respond (ri SPAHND) *v.* react to something that has been said or done **38**

select (suh LEKT) *v.* choose something or someone by carefully thinking about which is the best or most appropriate **45**

statistics (stuh TIS tiks) *n.* collection of numbers or data that represent facts or measurements **67**

suggest (suhg JEST) *v.* show indirectly; imply **15, 41**

support (suh POHRT) *v.* provide evidence to prove or back up an idea **15, 30**

tools (TOOLZ) *n.* any implement, instrument, or utensil used to do a particular job **8**

topic (TAHP ik) *n.* the subject **41, 62**

trivial (TRIV ee uhl) *adj.* of little importance **40**

utility (yoo TIL uh tee) *n.* the quality or property of being useful **74**

Photo Credits

Cover: Purestock/Getty Images; **iii: t.** © AP Photo/USPS; **iii: b.** © AP Photo; **4–5: t.** © Josh Westrich/zefa/Corbis; **b.** © AP Photo/Kevin Wolf; **6–7:** © Richard T. Nowitz/CORBIS; **9:** © AP Photo/The Free Lance-Star, Robert A. Martin; **10:** © AP Photo/Bebeto Matthews; **12–13:** © AP Photos/Kevin Wolf; **14:** © AP Photo/Egypt's Supreme Council of Antiquities/HO; **16–17:** © AP Photo/Paula Illingworth; **18:** © AP Photo/The Post and Courier, Alan Hawes; **20–21:** © AP Photo/The Post and Courier, Grace Beahm; **22: t.** © AP Photo; **22–23:** ©VO TRUNG DUNG/CORBIS SYGMA; **24:** © Robert P. Matthews/Princeton University/Getty Images; **27:** © Bettmann/CORBIS; **29:** © MPI/Getty Images; **31:** © AFP/Getty Images; **32:** © Stock Montage/Getty Images; **35:** © Imagno/Getty Images; **37:** © AP Photo/Lise Aserud/Scanpix/Pool; **40–41:** © Bill Ross/CORBIS; **41:** © Leonard de Selva/CORBIS; **43:** © Frank Cezus/Getty Images; **44:** © AP Photo/USPS; **47:** © AP Photo/HO/United States Postal Service; **48:** © AP Photo/USPS; **51: t.** © AP Photo/U.S. Postal Service; **51: b.** © AP Photo/USPS; **52–53:** © AP Photo/United States Postal Service, ho; **54–55:** © Eye-Stock/Alamy; **56:** © AP Photo/Pat Little; **58–59:** © Jerry Cooke/CORBIS; **59:** © AP Photo/Damian Dovarganes; **60:** © AP Photo/Reed Saxon; **62–63:** © AP Photo/Gail Oskin; **64:** © AP Photo/Apple, Handout; **69:** © Schlegelmilch/Corbis; **70–71:** © George Tiedemann/GT Images/Corbis; **73:** © C. Devan/zefa/Corbis; **74:** © Goodshoot/Corbis